Kids' Corner

Primary Rhymery

Sonja Dunn

Verlag an der Ruhr

IMPRESSUM

TITEL Kids' Corner – Primary Rhymery

AUTORIN Sonja Dunn

ILLUSTRATIONEN Jens Müller

LAYOUT/SATZ Jens Müller

DRUCK Druckerei Uwe Nolte, Iserlohn

VERLAG Verlag an der Ruhr
Postfach 10 22 51
45422 Mülheim an der Ruhr
Alexanderstraße 54
45472 Mülheim an der Ruhr
Tel.: 02 08 • 43 95 40
Fax: 02 08 • 439 5 439
E-Mail: info@verlagruhr.de
http://www.verlagruhr.de

ISBN 3-86072-588-2

Die Schreibweise der Texte folgt der reformierten Rechtschreibung.

Gedruckt auf chlorfrei gebleichtes Papier.

INHALT

Auf der beiliegenden CD finden Sie die Stücke in der hier angegebenen Reihenfolge.

VORWORT

„Wie kann man Kindern eine fremde Sprache näher bringen, ihnen eine positive Einstellung gegenüber anderen Sprachen und Kulturen vermitteln?“
Diese Kartei bietet Einsatzmöglichkeiten für unterschiedliche Themenbereiche – sei es im Rahmen des Begegnungssprachenunterrichts, des Englischunterrichts oder auch des interkulturellen Unterrichts.

Jeder kennt solche Situationen aus dem Urlaub, plötzlich soll Englisch gesprochen werden – und der Redefluss gerät trotz jahrelangen Englischunterrichts ins Stocken. In der Schule stehen die Vokabeln, die Grammatik, aber nicht das Sprechen der Alltagssprache im Vordergrund.
Anders als der herkömmliche Englischunterricht, der den Kindern die Sprache in kleinen Schritten beibringt, legt diese Kartei ihren Schwerpunkt auf das alltägliche Sprechen der Fremdsprache, auch wenn die Schüler dabei einige Wörter noch nicht kennen und sofort verstehen.

Die Gedichte von Sonja Dunn sind mitreißend. Sie laden zum Mitklatschen, Mitsprechen und Mitsingen ein. Auf der beiliegenden CD rezitiert die Autorin ihre Gedichte selbst. Der erste Kontakt mit einer Fremdsprache, d.h. mit einem richtigen „native speaker“, geschieht so auf spielerische Art und Weise und weckt die Lust an der neuen Sprache – Ohrwürmer sind garantiert.

Die Kartei enthält viele einfache kurze Gedichte und Reime, aber auch kompliziertere. Die Gedichte sind nach 18 verschiedenen Themenbereichen sortiert:
Begrüßung, Alltag, Unordnung/Aufräumen, Mein Körper, Lebensmittel/Ernährung, Weltraum/Fliegen, Ferien, Gesundheit/Krankheit, Freundschaft, Tiere, Gefühle/Stimmungen, Besondere Tage: Geburtstag/Weihnachten, Gruseln, Wetter, Umwelt, Rhythmus/Singen, Sport, Berufe.
Alle Bereiche haben ihren Platz in der Lebenswelt der Kinder.

Im Folgenden finden Sie einige Ideen und Anregungen zum Einsatz der Gedichte. Diese dienen nur als Beispiele – Sie können Ihrer eigenen Kreativität freien Lauf lassen!

Machen Sie es in Ihrer Klasse/Gruppe doch zu einem Ritual, sich auf Englisch zu begrüßen bzw. zu verabschieden. Das Lied **SAYING HELLO IS EASY** eignet sich dazu hervorragend. Es enthält keine schwierigen Wörter und hat eine einprägsame Melodie, die sich auch schon jüngere Kinder merken können.
Eine weitere Möglichkeit ist es, den Geburtstag eines Kindes mit einem englischsprachigen Geburtstagslied zu feiern. Hier bietet sich zum einen der Geburtstags-Rap **WHOSE BIRTHDAY IS IT?** an. Wenn die Kinder mit dem Sprechgesang vertraut sind, tauschen sie die dort verwendeten Namen einfach durch die Namen der Mitschüler aus.
Zum anderen kann das Stück **BIRTHDAYS** eingesetzt werden. Hier werden die Kinder aktiv: Sie klatschen mit den Händen, zucken die Schultern etc.

Ein Gedicht aus dem Bereich *Ferien* ist ein möglicher Aufhänger für den Austausch von Ferienplänen bzw. Ferienerlebnissen. Gerade vor Ferienbeginn lässt die Motivation der Kinder nach und nach den Ferien ist das Bedürfnis von Urlaubserlebnissen zu erzählen groß.
Durch das Lernen in Zusammenhängen prägen sich Vokabeln problemlos ein. Die Sprachkompetenz der Schüler wird erweitert.

VORWORT

Lassen Sie in den Sprachunterricht beispielsweise im Rahmen einer Grusel- oder Gedichtewerkstatt, englischsprachige Gedichte einfließen. Auf diese Weise lernen die Kinder mühelos Vokabeln und Aussprache. Geben Sie den Kindern Gelegenheit, die Gedichte vorzutragen. So lernen sie Gestik und Mimik einzusetzen. Das Selbstvertrauen der Kinder wird gestärkt.

Setzen Sie die Gedichte fächerübergreifend ein. Der Bereich *Tiere* kann zum Beispiel im Sprach- und Sachunterricht eingesetzt werden. Lassen Sie die Kinder zu den Gedichten **MY CAT**, **FAT CATS**, **PANTHERS AND LIONS**, **I WISH I HAD A DOG** etc. Bilder malen, die den entsprechenden Text wiedergeben. So setzen sich die Kinder kreativ mit den Texten auseinander.

Im Sprach- und Sachunterricht (natürlich auch in anderen Fächern) lassen sich u.a. die Gedichte zu den Themenbereichen *Berufe, Umwelt, Weltraum/Fliegen, Ernährung* einsetzen. So kann das Gedicht **HELPING** ein Einstieg in das Thema *Berufe* sein. Sprechen Sie, nach einer Klärung der englischen Begriffe, über die Notwendigkeit der einzelnen Berufe. Lassen Sie die Kinder im Anschluss daran von den Berufen ihrer Eltern berichten.

Beim Thema *Umwelt/Umweltschutz* kann das Gedicht **OUR PLANET** eingesetzt werden. Es ist sehr kurz und eignet sich besonders für jüngere Kinder. Der **ANTI-POLLUTION RAP** dagegen ist länger und komplizierter. Es enthält Hinweise darauf, wie man die Umwelt schützen kann. Sie können diese Gedichte als Themeneinstieg oder auch zum Abschluss einer Unterrichtsreihe nutzen. Es ist möglich, eines der Gedichte auf ein Plakat zu schreiben und den Hintergrund zu gestalten.

Im Zusammenhang mit dem Thema *Wetter* lässt sich u.a. das Gedicht **RAIN** vertonen. Lassen Sie die Kinder auf den Ausruf „Listen to the rain" überlegen (vielleicht auch heraushören), wie sich Regen anhört und durch welche Geräusche man Regen nachmachen kann. Spielen Sie das Gedicht anschließend mit Instrumenten, bzw. mit Geräuschen vor.

Passend zur Weihnachtszeit kann das Gedicht **HO HO HO** in das Projekt „Weihnachten in aller Welt" einfließen. Thematisieren Sie anhand dieses Gedichtes Unterschiede und Gemeinsamkeiten der weihnachtlichen Bräuche hier und in Amerika bzw. Kanada. Lassen Sie die Kinder beispielsweise auf einer Weihnachtsfeier verschiedene Gedichte zum Thema Weihnachten vortragen.

Der Bereich *Rhythmus/Singen* (aber auch die anderen Bereiche) bietet Lieder und Reime, die auch in den Musik- und Sportunterricht einfließen können. Viele Lieder, zum Beispiel **PUPPET!** und **RISE 'N SHINE**, lassen sich in Bewegung umsetzen und eignen sich als Auflockerung für zwischendurch, wenn die Konzentration nachlässt.

Die Stücke auf der CD entsprechen in der Regel den dazugehörigen Texten, wobei diese entweder gesprochen oder gesungen werden. Bei den Stücken **SAYING HELLO IS EASY**, **PUPPET!** und **CRACKERS AND CRUMBS** wird auf der CD nur die erste Strophe wiedergegeben. Das Gedicht **MCSPACE** wird von zwei Personen gesprochen, wobei jede Zeile einmal wiederholt wird.

So, und jetzt viel Spaß mit Primary Rhymery!

1 SAYING HELLO IS EASY

It's so easy to say hello
It's so easy to say hello
It's so easy to say hello
to say hello to you

It's so easy to shake a hand
It's so easy to shake a hand
It's so easy to shake a hand
to shake a hand with you

It's so easy to share some cake
It's so easy to share some cake
It's so easy to share some cake
to share some cake with you

It's so easy to tap a toe
It's so easy to tap a toe
It's so easy to tap a toe
to tap a toe with you

It's NOT easy to say goodbye
It's NOT easy to say goodbye
It's NOT easy to say goodbye
to say goodbye to you

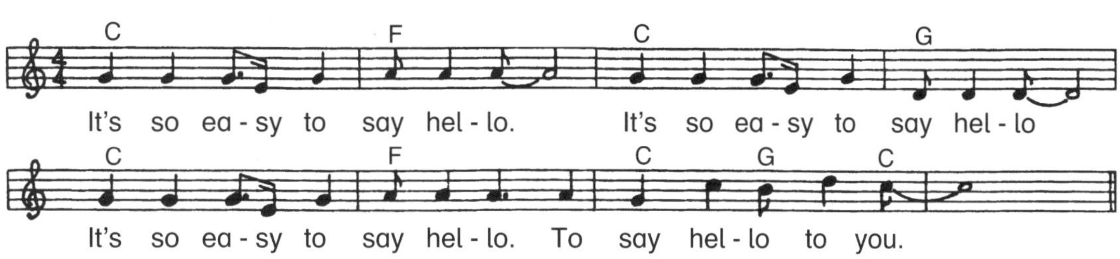

I WOKE UP IN THE MORNING

2

I woke up in the morning
and I jumped out of bed
put some clothes on my body
and a hat on my head
took a leap to the kitchen
and I ate my toast
listened to the news
from coast to coast
looked out the window
to check the sun
ran out the door
to have some fun

MAGIC WORDS

3

Thank you
Please
Excuse me
You're welcome
If you please
Pardon me
Don't mention it
Magic words are these

4 THE SHARING RAP

Now listen to my story
'bout a not nice guy
He never shares his sandwich
or his apple pie
He keeps all his lunches
safely hid
Man, he's some, mean
stingy kid

5 LISTEN

Listen to the noise
Listen to the noise
Listen to the noise
made by those boys!

YOW!

UNORDNUNG AUFRÄUMEN

6 KATY

Katy Sticky Fingers
Smudges on the wall
Crumbs along the carpet
In the upstairs hall

7 STORE ROOM

My own bedroom's
like a store
since I dumped
my dresser drawer

Piles of T shirts
on the floor
A hundred sox
or maybe more

I'm a salesman
I'm a clerk
Selling clothes is
quite hard work

Now I've changed
I'm buying pants
Show me some, please
for a dance

Have you any special shoes?
A jumping pair
for me to choose?

Here comes Grandad
to my store
trying mittens
from the floor

Mommy's head peeks
'round my door
„PUT THOSE CLOTHES BACK
IN YOUR DRAWER!“

8 CRACKERS AND CRUMBS

Crackers and crumbs
Crackers and crumbs
These are my fingers
These are my thumbs
These are my eyes
These are my ears
They'll all grow big
in the next ten years

Crackers and cheese
Crackers and cheese
These are my elbows
These are my knees
This is my mouth
This is my nose
When I tell a lie
it grows and it grows

9 FUNNY FACE

Where oh where
did you get that face
that face
that face
that funny funny face?
I got it at the
face-painting place

10 CHEERS FOR FLAVORS

We got a C
We got an H
We got an E-R-R-Y
We got a CHERRY CHERRY
CHERRY pie
Cherries are red
Cherries are sweet
Cherry pies are good to eat

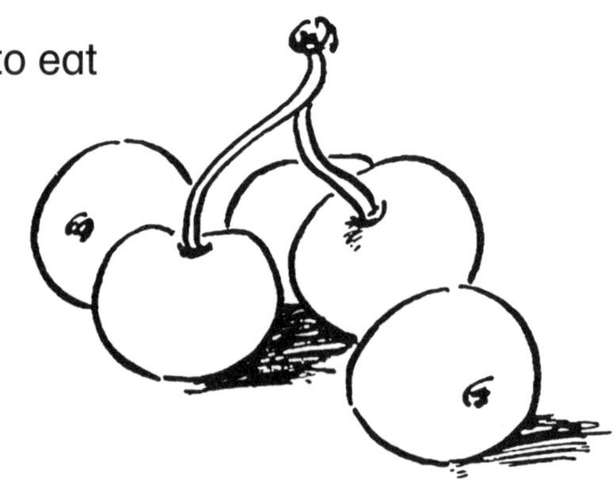

11 CHEESE CHEER

Cheddar
Gouda
Mozzarella

White cheese
Blue cheese
Even yella

Swiss cheese
Marble
Parmesan

Eat it up
until it's gone

12 MAKING PIZZA

Gonna make pizza
Gonna make it fast

Gonna eat it slowly
Gonna make it last

Gonna add tomatoes
Pepperoni too

Gonna make pizza
And share it with you

13 PIZZA AND POP

Pizza and pop
Pizza and pop
When I get started
I just can't stop
The smell is delicious
The taste extra yummy
I love it the most
when it gets to my tummy

14 JUNK FOOD

Junk food
Junk food
I love junk food
I eat junk food
I can't stop

Reese's pieces
Greasy French fries
Caramel popcorn
Soda pop

Sticky candy
Gooey choc'late
Salted cheesies
Sugared glop

Junk food
Junk food
I love junk food
I eat junk food
till I drop!

15 HOT DOGS FOREVER

Hot dogs for breakfast
Hot dogs for lunch
Hot dogs
Hot dogs
all in a bunch

You can eat 'em with mustard
You can eat 'em with cheese
You can eat 'em
any way you please

Eat 'em from the Bar-B-Q
Eat 'em from the pot
Eat 'em cold or
Eat 'em hot
Eat 'em standing up
or down on your knees

Hot dogs
Hot dogs
Please Please Please

16 GOOD „EATS"

Cookies in the car
Cookies in the car
Somebody stole them
from the cookie jar
Crumbs on the dashboard
Crumbs on the seat
Cookies taste the best
and are the best to eat

17 TONIONS OF ONIONS

Tonions of onions
for us to eat
Tonions of onions
around our feet
Tonions of onions
a scrumptious treat
They fell from a truck
that turned onto our street

WELTRAUM FLIEGEN

18 MCSPACE

McMoon
McVenus
McMars
A hamburger stand in the stars
Fly into McSpace and
fill your McFace and
take a McSwing
on McStars

VENUS

MOON

MARS

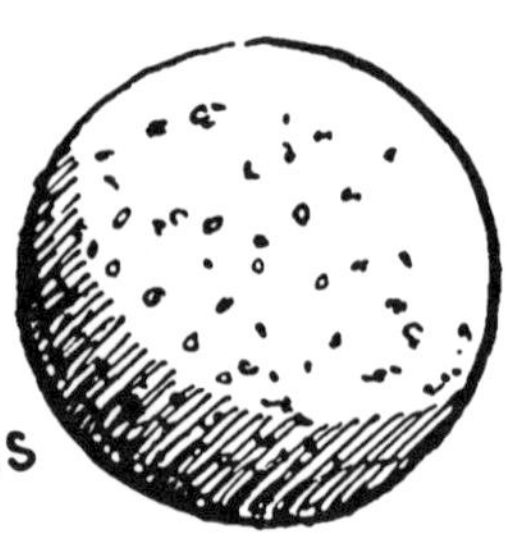

19 STARS ON MARS

Are there stars on Mars?
Do they play guitars?
Do they eat nut bars
and mints in jars?
Do they drive big cars
or minotaurs?
Can they make big scars
with scimitars?
These stars on Mars
These stars on Mars

WELTRAUM FLIEGEN

20 FLYING

Would you go into orbit
if you were invited
on a silver shuttle
with lunch provided?

Would you guzzle a malted
from the milky pathway
and not phone your mother
for the whole long day?

Would you fly to Saturn?
Would you streak to Mars?
Then would you jet back home
on the shooting stars?

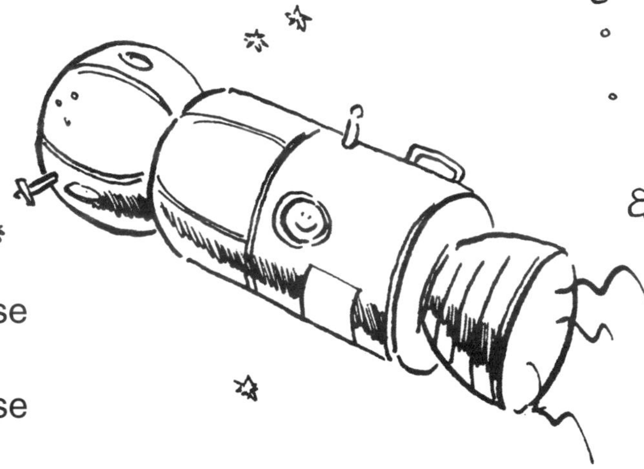

21 BROTHERHOOD

Fly, fly, fly ’round the universe
Fly, fly, fly ’round the earth
Fly, fly, fly ’round the universe
Fly, fly, fly ’round the earth

My feathers touch my brother
My feathers touch my sister
Circle, circle, circle, circle
Circle to my brother

Fly, fly, fly ’round the universe
Fly, fly, fly ’round the earth

HOLIDAYS

22

Driving to the cottage
You can come too
Going to stay a week
for a Bar-B-Q
Fishing and
swimming and
surfing too
Looking for bears
and
a heron blue

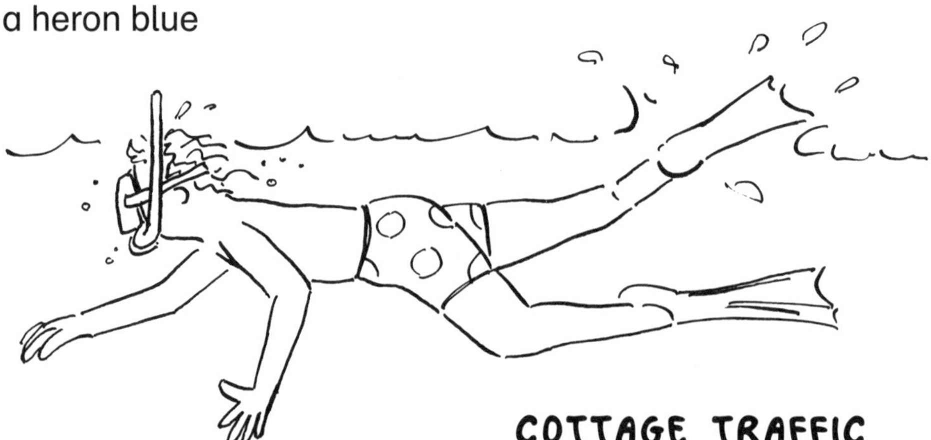

COTTAGE TRAFFIC

23

Driving
from the cottage
late at night
See a looooong
red
tail
of lights
Slow as a snail
Bumper to bumper to bumper
to bumper
Grownups say it's a bore
I love watching
this red S N A K E

24 KEEPING FIT

Mike Mike
Ride that bike

Rose Rose
Kiss your toes

Joe Joe
Start to row

Jack Jack
Run the track

Di Di
Touch the sky

Peg Peg
Shake a leg

Paul Paul
Kick the ball

Jim Jim
Get in the swim

Kate Kate
Swirl and skate

Ann Marie
You'd better ski

Dennis Dennis
Play some tennis

Make a hit by
keeping fit!

25 EVERY SIX MONTHS

I went to the dentist
to get checked out
The dentist said, „Kelly
open your mouth.
You've brushed and flossed
after eating cheese.
That's why you have
NO CAVITIES."

26 I'VE GOT A COLD

I've got a cold
And I don't like it
No, I don't like it
Not one bit

When you catch a cold
and it's in your head
your nose gets plugged
and your eyes turn red

You can't taste your food
'cause it hurts your throat
Your ears get plugged
and you can't sing a note

You cough and sneeze
and gasp and wheeze

You have a fever
That weakens your knees

There isn't much that you can do
but keep yourself warm
and drink a hot brew

And sleep a lot when you get into bed —
Just pull those covers
right over your head

27 POX PAIN

Chicken pox
Chicken pox
Hate them worse than
dirty socks

28 BRIAN

Brian lost his front tooth
in the strangest way
He was eating ice cream
after school one day
He bit down on a walnut
and then let out a roar
„Hey Mommy,
check this hole out
that wasn't there before!"

29 MY FRIEND

Who's the one
who talks to me?
My friend

Who's the one
who walks with me?
My friend

Who's the one
who shares his pie?
My friend

Who doesn't mind it
when I cry?
My friend

Who's always with me
in the park?
My friend

Who holds my hand
when it gets dark?
My friend
My friend
My friend

30 I'LL BE YOUR FRIEND

I'll be your friend
for as long as you like
I'll share all my candy
I'll lend you my bike

We'll go to the movies
We'll play in the park
I'll hold your hand tightly
when we walk in the dark

I'll hug you hard
if you ever cry
and give you half
of my Mile High Pie

Together we'll be
Together we'll be
very best friends
just you and me

FRIENDS

31

Are you French
Are you Dutch
Are you Macedonian
Or British
Or Greek
Or Patagonian?
Maybe you're Irish
or Welsh
or Iranian
Danish
or Yiddish

Perhaps you're Ukrainian
Italian or Spanish
Perchance you're American
African
Mexican
Native Canadian
You could be Chinese
Pakistani
or Asian

Lebanese
Portuguese
Wherever will it end?

No matter what you are
you'll always be my friend!

32 MY CAT

My cat can stalk
My cat can walk
But how I wish
my cat could
TALK!

33 FAT CATS

Mumbo and Jumbo
were two fat cats
They ran around the house
and chased all the rats

34 SPECIAL DIET

There's something wrong with Sasha
He doesn't want to purr
His motor isn't running
And all because of her

Her name is little Myshka
a teeny tiny mouse
She's peeking out at Sasha
who can't get in her house

He's posted by her doorway
a hole where he won't fit
He doesn't want his dinner
and all he does is sit

The same old dried up cat food
is all that's in the house
It isn't appetizing
when Sasha wants some „mouse"

35 MEI LING

She's a cranky old kitty
but I love her so
She spits and hisses
when she steps in the snow
She can't stand children
'cause they poke and they tease
„Don't bother me, baby,
I'm Siamese!"

36 BIG WIDE WORLD

Big wide world
Big wide world

What shall we see in
the big wide world?

Shall we see a chicken
peep, peep, peep?

Yes, we'll see a chicken
peep, peep, peep

Shall we see a duckling
quack, quack, quack?

Yes, we'll see a duckling
quack, quack, quack

Shall we see a robin
chirp, chirp, chirp?

Yes, we'll see a robin
chirp, chirp, chirp

Big wide world
Big wide world

What shall we see in
the big wide world?

Shall we see a . . .

37 PANTHERS AND LIONS

Panthers and lions
Panthers and lions
They're at the zoo
Just look for the signs.

38 MY DOG JAY

Ruggle dee
Buggle dee
My dog Jay
guards my house
both night and day
Robbers, prowlers
stay away
You'll get scared
by my dog Jay

39 I WISH I HAD A DOG

I wish I had a dog
A great big dog
A dog I could call my own
I'd feed him
I'd please him
I never would tease him
I'd give him a great big bone.

40 WHO'S A SCAREDY CAT?

I never met a dragon
that I didn't like
Especially a dragon
riding on a trike

I never met a tiger
that I didn't pet
Especially a tiger
whose nose was cool and wet

I never met a bunyip
at whom I didn't wave
Especially while walking
past a darkened cave

I never met a dinosaur
at whom I didn't smile
Especially a dinosaur
closer than a mile

41 SAURUSES

Mommysaurus
Daddysaurus
Babysaurus too
went for a walk
to the city zoo
They growled at the tigers
They yelled at the yaks
They squealed at the elephants
and jumped upon their backs
They drank popsaurus
They ate saurus-steaks
They gobbled junkosaurus food
and home they went
with tummy aches

42 BAD MOOD RAP

When you come home
from school
and you're in a bad mood
and your parents say,
„Come and eat your food"
and you don't feel hungry
and you don't feel nice
the last thing you want
is their advice
you just feel you want to
kick the cat
or lie on your bed
in your favorite hat
or stay in your room
stare at the wall
and not talk to anyone at all
And if people call you
on the phone
you holler out loud,
„Why don't you
leave me alone!"
You're as cross as a bear
and as mad as a snake
and you feel like cussin'
for goodness' sake

Well, hold on a minute
if you would
You're just in a very
frightful mood
So frightful you can
almost cry
and holy smoke
you don't know why
Well, lots of times
we all feel like that
Feel like we want to
kick the cat
and slam the door
on poor old Rover

But cheer up my friend
It'll soon be over

43 BABYSITTERS

They never ask ME
if I'm allowed
That really makes me mad
They always say, „Ask his parents!"
So they ask my Mom or Dad
„Is HE allowed a piece of cake?
Is HE allowed TV?
Is HE allowed to go outside
or climb the apple tree?
Is HE allowed to ride his bike
or cross the road with Jed?"

But they never ask my parents
if I'm allowed to go to bed!

44 PRACTICE PAIN

Piano lessons
Piano lessons
Sitting on the stool
Piano lessons
Piano lessons
Practice after school
Piano lessons
Piano lessons
Practice every day

I don't want to practise
I JUST WANT TO PLAY

45 WHOSE BIRTHDAY IS IT?

Is this the birthday party?
Uh Huh
Is this the birthday party?
Uh Huh
Is everybody here?
Uh Huh
Is Andy here?
Uh Huh
Is Brian here?
Uh Huh
Is Hosa here?
Uh Huh
Is Deborah here?
Uh Huh
Is Ellen here?
Uh Huh
Is Francis here?
Uh Huh
Is Gordie here?
Uh Huh
Is Heidi here?
Uh Huh
Is Ivan here?
Uh Huh
Is Jimmy here?
Uh Huh
Is Kevin here?
Uh Huh

Is Lisa here?
Uh Huh
Is Marty here?
Uh Huh
Is Nadine here?
Uh Huh
Is Oryst here?
Uh Huh
Is Penny here?
Uh Huh
Is Quentin here?
Uh Huh
Is Ronnie here?
Uh Huh
Is Sonja here?
Uh Huh
Is Tommy here?
Uh Huh
Is Una here?
Uh Huh
Is Vera here?
Uh Huh
Is Willie here?
Uh Huh
Is Yuri here?
Uh Huh
Is Zenon here?
Uh Huh
WHOSE BIRTHDAY IS IT?
Kevin's
HAPPY BIRTHDAY, KEVIN!
Thank you
Is everybody hungry?
Uh Huh!
LET'S EAT!

BESONDERE TAGE:

GEBURTSTAG WEIHNACHTEN

46 BIRTHDAYS

Hey, Hey
when's your Birthday?

Clap your hands
if it's January

Stamp your feet
if it's February

Shrug your shoulders
if it's March

If it's April
up you stand

Born in May
wave your hand

June's the month
to touch the sky

Fly around
if it's July

If it's August
blow your nose

In September
touch those toes

If your day is in October
start that day
by rolling over

In November
bend your knees

Here's December
you must freeze!

47 HO, HO, HO

What does Santa say
as he flies through the
snow?
Merry merry Christmas
HO HO HO

What does Santa say
to make his reindeer go?
Merry merry Christmas
HO HO HO

48 DANCE OF THE BONES

old bones rattling
yellow teeth snapping
bald head wagging
arms flip flopping
long legs clicking
knee bones knocking
skipping prancing
’round the room
’round and ’round and
’round the room

crickety crack
down and back
bones hopping
bones dropping
pieces popping
’round the room
’round and ’round and
’round the room

’round and ’round and
’round the room

49 BOIL THE BATS

Boil the bats
Stir in rats
snakes and scales
slippery tails
and here’s for you
a witch’s brew!

50 NO WELCOME HERE

Rattling bones
Squeaking doors
Dusty cobwebs
Creaking floors
Spooky ghosts
Chestnut roasts
Haunted castles
Freezing moats
Snarling cats
Flitting bats . . .
Never cross
*un*welcome mats

51 HERE COMES THE WITCH

Here comes the witch
so don't get caught!
She'll bake you in the oven!
She'll boil you in the pot!

THE BLANKET DOESN'T FEEL RIGHT

52

I heard a noise in the basement
It gave me quite a fright!
And I don't want to go to bed now
'cause the blanket doesn't feel right

On a scary night, on a scary night
the blanket doesn't feel right!

I saw a creepy shadow
It was a spooky sight!
And I don't want to go to bed now
'cause the blanket doesn't feel right

On a scary night, on a scary night
the blanket doesn't feel right!

There's someone in the attic
It's dark and there's no light!
And I don't want to go to bed now
'cause the blanket doesn't feel right

On a scary night, on a scary night
the blanket doesn't feel right!

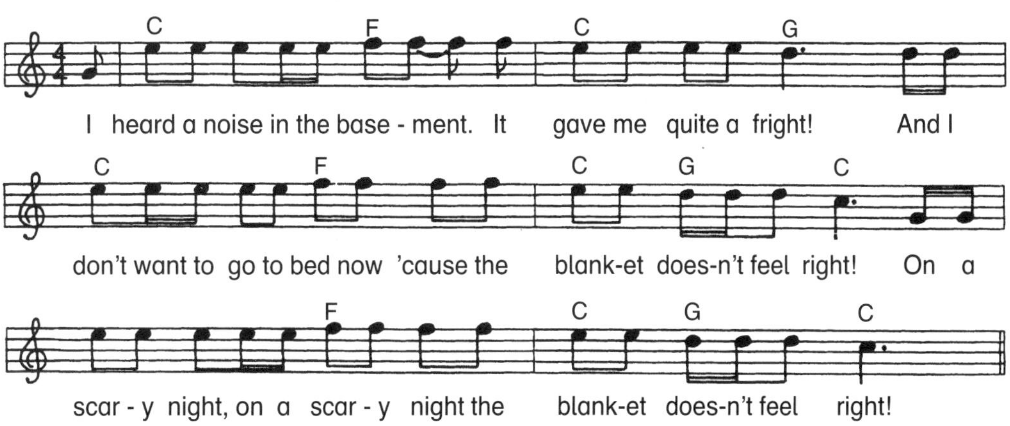

52

53 DIFFERENT DAYS

Rainy rainy day
Rainy rainy day
We'll all get wet
on a rainy rainy day

Sunny sunny day
Sunny sunny day
We'll all go swimming
on a sunny sunny day

Snowy snowy day
Snowy snowy day
We'll all go sledding
on a snowy snowy day

Icy icy day
Icy icy day
We'll all go skating
on an icy icy day

Frosty frosty day
Frosty frosty day
We'll freeze our noses
on a frosty frosty day

54 LOTSA WINDS

How many sounds
do the four winds make?

Hundreds and hundreds
for goodness' sake

Listen listen
to the sound
as they whoosh
around and 'round

Missssssssssssstral
SSSSSSSSSSSSSirocco
ChChChChChChChinooooook
Monssoooooooooooooooooon
Doldruuuuuuuuuuuuuuuum
Traaaaaaaaaaade wiiiiiiind
Northsouthwesteast wiiiiiiinds
ZZZZZZZZZZZZZZZZZephyr

If you make those sounds again
you may start a HURRICANE!

55 RAIN

listen listen
listen to the rain
listen listen
listen to the rain
listen listen listen listen
listen to the rain

softer softer
listen to the rain
softer softer
listen to the rain
listen listen listen listen
listen to the rain

louder louder
listen to the rain
louder louder
listen to the rain
listen listen listen listen
listen to the rain

56 RAINBOW

Please don't rush me, Daddy
I want to taste the sun
I want to climb the rainbow
now that the storm is done

57 BE PREPARED

Slippery
Sloppery
Slushery snow
Do up your snowshoes
and let's go

Drippery
Droppery
Drizzery rain
Open your „yella“ umbrella
again

Mistery
Moistery
Mustery fog
Make sure you have
a strong leash for your dog

58 SHAKING OUT SILLIES

If the wind blows your umbrella
completely inside out
run between the raindrops
and shake your sillies out

59 OUR PLEA

Save our land
Save our fish
Save our deer
That's our wish

60 ANTI-POLLUTION RAP

Don't throw your garbage
out on the street
You gotta
keep your planet
clean and neat
Put your wrappers
in the big round bin
Recycle cans
that are made of tin
Take your bottles
back to the store
Get a refund
to buy some more
Never toss junk
from a moving auto
'cause „Clean is keen"
should be your motto

61 PUPPET!

Puppet, can you clap your hands
Clap your hands
Clap your hands
Puppet, can you clap your hands
Clap your hands like this?

Oh yes, I can clap my hands
Clap my hands
Clap my hands
Oh yes, I can clap my hands
Clap my hands like this

Puppet, can you scratch your ear
Scratch your ear
Scratch your ear
Puppet, can you scratch your ear
Scratch your ear like this?

Oh yes, I can scratch my ear
Scratch my ear
Scratch my ear
Oh yes, I can scratch my ear
Scratch my ear like this

Puppet, can you bow down low
Bow down low
Bow down low
Puppet, can you bow down low
Bow down low like this?

Oh, yes, I can bow down low
Bow down low
Bow down low
Oh yes, I can bow down low
Bow down low like this

Puppet, can you shake your head
Shake your head
Shake your head
Puppet, can you shake your head
Shake your head like this?

Oh yes, I can shake my head
Shake my head
Shake my head
Oh yes, I can shake my head
Shake my head like this

Puppet, can you wave goodbye
Wave goodbye
Wave goodbye
Puppet, can you wave goodbye
Wave goodbye like this?

Oh yes, I can wave goodbye
Wave goodbye
Wave goodbye
Oh yes, I can wave goodbye
Wave goodbye like this

Oh yes, I can clap my hands
Scratch my ear
Bow down low
Shake my head
And wave goodbye like this

62 THINGS PUPPETS CAN DO

A puppet in my pocket
A puppet in my hat
A puppet can do many things
Now, what do you think of that?

My puppet can say, „Yes Ma'am."
My puppet can say, „No!"
My puppet says, „That's yummy."
Or, „Sorry, I don't know."

My puppet walks quite slowly
And bows down very low
My puppet slides and runs fast
„Good-bye! It's time to go."

63 RISE 'N SHINE

You gotta rise and shine
in the morning
rise and shine
at noon
Rise 'n Shine
Rise 'n Shine
Suppertime will be here soon

You gotta rise and shine
at breakfast
rise and shine
at lunch
Rise 'n Shine
Rise 'n Shine
Everybody in a bunch

You gotta rise and shine
rise and shine
Everybody in a bunch

64 RHYTHM AND RHYME

There's a rhythm in the air
There's a rhythm everywhere

There's a rhythm in the land
There's a rhythm in the band
There's a rhythm on the street

There's a rhythm in my feet
There's a rhythm in the stream
There's a rhythm in my dream

There's a rhythm in my walk
There's a rhythm in my talk
There's a rhythm in my toes

And it goes and goes and goes
There's a rhythm in the sea

There's a rhythm in ME!

65 COCONUT WARNING RAP

Now, here's a little warning
So listen to me
Never ever sit beneath
a coconut tree
They're great for drinking
They're fine for percussion
But if one hits your head
you'll get a concussion

66 TENNIS EVERYONE

Upcourt
Downcourt
Sideways too
Forehand
Backhand
Lobby loo
Ace one
Place one
Don't disgrace one
Tennis is the game
for me and
for you

67 SPORTS

Soccer in the morning
and in the afternoon
Playing for the A team
Gonna beat 'em soon

68 HELPING

All the people in our town
help to make the world go 'round

Judge
Professor
Hair dresser

Cook
Hatter
Baseball batter

Priest
Musician
Obstetrician

Nurse
Lawyer
Bug destroyer

Dentist
Writer
Firefighter

These are only but a few
See if you can rhyme some too

69 THE FIREFIGHTER

Who's the bravest man about
the one who puts the fires out
the one who climbs the ladders tall
and rescues kittens from the wall?

Put down those matches!
Drop that lighter!
Don't make work for
the FIREFIGHTER!

70 TEACHERS

Teachers do this
and teachers do that
And teachers pull rabbits
out of a hat

Teachers sing songs
and teachers are good
Teachers play dress-up
in cape and hood

Teachers mark papers
Teachers tie boots
listen to screaming
hollers and hoots

71 DOCTOR, DOCTOR

Doctor, doctor
get here quick
My favorite dolly
is sick, sick, sick
She's got the sniffles
She's got the flu
She's even got
the doodle de doo
I gave her syrup
and chicken soup
and now she's come down
with the croup
So, doctor, please
don't mind the weather
Come right now
and make her better

72 HARD AT WORK

Diggers and cranes
Diggers and cranes
The workers work hard
But they rest when it rains

LITERATUR-VERZEICHNIS

Bye, Chris: **Kinder lernen Englisch**
The world around us.
Verlag an der Ruhr. 2001. **ISBN 3-86072-596-3**

Bye, Chris: **Kinder lernen Englisch**
Colours, Numbers, ABC, Day and Night, Fun and Games.
Verlag an der Ruhr. 2001. **ISBN 3-86072-597-1**

Moser, Franz; Binder, Vera u.a.: **Learn English – just sing!**
Veritas; Cornelsen. 1999. **ISBN 3-464-21810-4**
Englisch lernen mit Liedern für Kinder von 6-10 Jahren.
Motivierende Unterrichtsmaterialien mit Methode.

Powell, Richard: **888 Wörter Englisch: Ein Bildwörterbuch.**
Carlsen. 2000. **ISBN 3-551-13470-7**
Eine Sammlung von englischen Grundbegriffen
in engl.-dtsch. und dtsch.-engl.

Raab, Dorothee; Klenovsky, Kerstin: **Spaß mit Englisch.**
Carlsen. 2000. **ISBN 3-551-13825-7**
Spiele und Rätsel für Englisch in der Grundschule.

Rohrauer, Christine und Josef: **Englisch in der Grundschule**.
Veritas; Cornelsen. 1994. **ISBN 3-464-21620-9**
Praktische Tipps für den Englischunterricht.

Schmidt, Katja: **First Steps into English.** (Kid's corner).
Verlag an der Ruhr. 2000. **ISBN 3-86072-580-7**
Zahlreiche Kopiervorlagen und praktische Tipps
für den Englischunterricht in der Grundschule.

Tokes, Reka: **Kid's stuff – Spielen, singen, sprechen.**
Verlag an der Ruhr. 1999. **ISBN 3-86072-438-X**
Ansprechend gestaltete Unterrichtsmaterialien mit Reimen,
Liedern, bekannten Gesellschaftsspielen, Situations- und
Bewegungsspielen, die den Englischunterricht
zu einem Kinderspiel machen.

Verlag an der Ruhr

www.verlagruhr.de

Katja Schmidt

Kids' Corner: First steps into English

11 Einheiten zu Themen aus dem Kinderalltag führen die Kinder schrittweise an die englische Sprache heran. Zahlreiche Kopiervorlagen mit Rätseln, Bildern, Lückentexten und Spielen machen den Englischunterricht easy.

Ab Klasse 2, 75 S., A4, Papph.
ISBN 3-86072-580-7
Best.-Nr. 2580
36,- DM/sFr/263,-öS

Chris Bye

Kids' Corner: Kinder lernen Englisch mit Ella Elephant Colors, Numbers, ABC, Day and Night, Fun and Games

Zahlreiche Aktivitäten zu den Themenbereichen: Farben, Zahlen, Buchstaben und Uhrzeit. Anschauliche Illustrationen, Basteltipps und Kopiervorlagen begleiten die thematischen Einheiten. Mit diesen Materialien sind Sie bestens ausgerüstet. Let´s speak English!

Ab Kl. 2, 40 S., A4, Papph.
ISBN 3-86072-597-1
Best.-Nr. 2597
31,20 DM/sFr/228,- öS

Reka Tokes

Kids' stuff – Spielen, singen, sprechen

Zahlreiche Materialien für den Englischunterricht in der Grundschule: Reime, Lieder, Gesellschaftsspiele, Bastelbögen, Bewegungsspiele und Bilder ermöglichen ein spielerisches Erlernen der neuen Sprache.

Klasse 1 - 4, 92 S., A4, Papph.
ISBN 3-86072-438-X
Best.-Nr. 2438
38,- DM/sFr/277,- öS

Chris Bye

Kids' Corner: Kinder lernen Englisch mit Harry Horse The World Around Us

Englischunterricht einmal anders. Verschiedene Themen aus der Alltagswelt schaffen Situationen, in denen die Kinder handeln und die neue Sprache aktiv sprechen. Die Fingerpuppen Harry Horse und der Elefant Ella begleiten sie dabei. Mit Kopiervorlagen, Basteltipps und Illustrationen.

Ab Kl. 2, 40 S., A4, Papph.
ISBN 3-86072-596-3
Best.-Nr. 2596
31,20 DM/sFr/228,- öS

kreativ

spielerisch

lernen

Jackie Silberg

Aber ich kann doch gar nicht singen!

Musik ist Rhythmus, Musik ist Sprache und Musik ist Geräusch – mit vielen Spielvorschlägen und Ideen wird hier Musik unterrichten leicht gemacht.

Ab Kl. 1, 175 S., 16 x 23 cm, Pb.
ISBN 3-86072-444-4
Best.-Nr. 2444
28,- DM/sFr/204,- öS

Laurie Carlson

Wie die Indianer wirklich lebten

Über 100 Aktivitäten, die den Kindern das wirkliche Leben der Indianer näher bringen. Die Kinder fertigen Kleidungsstücke und Schmuck an, kochen indianische Gerichte und stellen wichtige Alltagsgegenstände her.

8 - 11 J., 190 S., A4-quer, Pb.
ISBN 3-86072-566-1
Best.-Nr. 2566
39,80 DM/sFr/291,- öS
(erscheint 4. Quartal 2000)

Jakobine Wirtz

Aber ich kann doch gar nicht malen!

Ob Sie Farben benutzen oder mit Formen experimentieren, auf Tapete oder Pappe malen: Mit Hilfe der genauen Anleitungen zu den verschiedensten Techniken wird die Kreativität der Kinder in Ihrem Kunstunterricht stetig wachsen.

Ab Kl. 1, 177 S., 16 x 23 cm, Pb.
ISBN 3-86072-562-9
Best.-Nr. 2562
29,80 DM/sFr/218,- öS

Laurie Carlson

Der wahre Wilde Westen

Über 100 Aktivitäten, die den Kindern helfen, das Land der Cowboys und Siedler Nordamerikas kennenzulernen. Die Kinder basteln, kochen, spielen und entdecken so den Wilden Westen wie er wirklich war.

8 - 11 J., 150 S., A4-quer, Pb.
ISBN 3-86072-567-X
Best.-Nr. 2567
38,- DM/sFr/277,- öS
(erscheint 4. Quartal 2000)

Verlag an der Ruhr

Postfach 10 22 51 · D-45422 Mülheim an der Ruhr
Tel.: 02 08/49 50 40 · Fax: 02 08/495 0495
e-mail: info@verlagruhr.de

Bücher für die pädagogische Praxis